THE LIVING-LOVING GENERATION

THE
LIVING-LOVING
GENERATION

edited by

DAN and ROSE LUCEY

THE BRUCE PUBLISHING COMPANY / Milwaukee

NIHIL OBSTAT:

RICHARD J. SKLBA, S.S.L., S.T.D.
Censor librorum

IMPRIMATUR:

✠ WILLIAM E. COUSINS
Archbishop of Milwaukee
November 16, 1968

The poems by Chris Lucey used in this book, are reproduced with the permission of PREFACE, student magazine of the University of Portland, where they first appeared.

The serigraph in the chapter headings is by Sister Marie Vincent Brothers. The serigraph used on the jacket is by Sister Mary Gerold Mobley.

Library of Congress Catalog Card Number: 69-17322

Copyright © 1969 THE BRUCE PUBLISHING COMPANY
MADE IN THE UNITED STATES OF AMERICA

From a College Dorm

My soul screams
for what?
it does not know.

"I am written out"
said the joker to the spade
"for the night".

"So stop writing writing"
he said in a reversal of roles.

EDITORS' PREFACE

Teenage is great
Teenage is exciting
Teenage is gross
Teenage is living
Teenage is loving
Teenage is saying "yes"

Take your choice. Dissecting teen-agers has become a national pastime. Never before in the history of our country has the growing-up process of a generation of young people commanded so much attention. There are many reasons for this. The teen-years have evolved into a special-category group formerly unknown. Youngsters used to live very close to the small family circle until their college years, or until they married. The changing pattern of family life and the growing importance of the communications media changed much of this by forming a separate cult of teen-age.

John and Mary, Dick and Jane historically went through the process of passing from childhood into adulthood with many aches and pains. The fact of facing adulthood and its responsibilities through a process of reaching out and retreating is not new; what is new is that instead of the growing up being done by individuals, it is now being done as a chorus. The young adult has become to many people just a part of a small mob which threatens them. The cult which compels youngsters to rock with the latest music, spend their time riding the surf, strumming guitars, skiing the slopes, or all four, scares some people to death. The ability of young people to stack records to the ceiling, to spend millions of dollars on clothes and cars is a phenomenon new for an America which learned well the maxim "a penny saved is a penny earned" and "idle hands are the devil's workshop."

What we see as exciting and revolutionary about the new teens is their desire and willingness to reach out of themselves to love people everywhere, to respond to the challenge of growing up in one of the most demanding and frustrating periods in history.

Around the country a living, loving generation is saying "yes" to the needs and aspirations of other men. In the urban areas there are young people tutoring deprived children, involving themselves in politics, working with migrant workers, joining the Peace Corps, AID, and Vista. This deep concern among the teenagers for justice and love is, too, a new cycle in our national life; one to be admired and encouraged.

Reality demands honesty. The teen years are like other periods of our life; a time of trial, success, and failure. Living is growing, and all of growth is change. We live and love and change and grow day by day; our only fear should be of being alive and of not living. This book, we hope, is about living and growing. It is an attempt on the part of the various writers, who span a generation of living and loving, to communicate many points of view about becoming persons and about squaring this becoming with their own charts of life. Some of the charts have already been tested and lived; others are being tried by a Living-Loving Generation who know that "You risk crying when you let yourself love." The reader will use the chapters to open his own vistas in the direction he chooses.

Dan and Rose Lucey

CONTRIBUTORS' PROFILE

Ann Brassier—educated in Southern California and Atchison, Kansas
(Mt. St. Scholastica, '67). American College Who's Who '66, '67.
Editor *Mount Mirror,* 1966. Interagency Recruiter, U.S. Civil
Service Commission, St. Louis Region.

Tina Cole—Sociology major, University of San Francisco, '68. Shared
her pad with six brothers and sisters, summer counsellor on
East Coast. Will work in Europe a year before teaching on
West Coast.

Rev. James R. Anderson—Author, Director CARA, Washington, D.C.
Director Leadership Training Program. Pastor, Community of
St. Paul, experimental parish in diocese of Stockton, Calif.

Dr. Joseph and Lois Bird—authors of best-selling *The Freedom Of
Sexual Love* and *Love Is All.* Dr. Bird is a clinical psychologist
and psychotherapist in Saratoga, Calif.

Jerry and Geraldine Raffo—Alumni of San Francisco State and University of San Francisco respectively; parents of tiny Cecelia and
Theresa. Jerry is an expert in Government Bonds; Geraldine a
speech therapist. Both work in Search Program and Oakland
Diocesan T-V.

Pat and Patty Crowley—Chicago founders of Christian Family Movement, confidants of families on every continent, members Papal
Commission on Population, Director Fund for Republic, only
couple to receive Laetare Medal from the University of Notre
Dame.

Dr. Willis McNelly—Professor in English Department, California
State College, Fullerton. With his wife, Genevieve, CFM leaders
in Archdiocese of Los Angeles and pioneers in Adult Education,
St. Joseph's College, Orange, Calif.

THE INSIDE

THE LIVING-LOVING GENERATION

1

BEiNG iS BECOMiNG

Ann Lucey Brassier

Say your name. Listen to someone else call you. It's a good sound because it singles you out from everyone else. It's yours alone. It is a word that you have recognized ever since you can remember, a sound you have always responded to, but who is the individual who is behind that name? Who *are* you? Perhaps you're short with dark hair and big brown eyes, or you're almost skinny with a sandy crew cut. And you are much more. Right now you may not even realize how much more there is to you. You may be aware of the great variety of feelings and thoughts and sighs and screams that come from different parts of you, but so far you don't see much rhyme and reason to it all—or do you? All the parts don't fit together into a single whole, a person that you *know* is *you*, that you can be proud of and happy to live with. The time must come, though, when you can hear your name and know what it represents. You must know yourself completely and be proud of ME.

There is no easy formula for drawing all the strings together into one well-tied knot. I know who I am, but I can remember the time when there were so many versions of me that I never knew what to expect from me next. Knowing what to expect next is an important part of being yourself, too. You can't live with a person who is completely unpredictable, nor with a will and heart which are always pulling in opposite directions. You can't live with a person who always does things that confuse you, or make you ashamed. It is great to live with someone you really love and understand. Yet there is no formula for becoming such a person because each one must work it out for himself.

I could tell you how I did it, but looking back I see no clear pattern; I just see life—life, changing, retreating, advancing—and me.

It is even difficult to set a goal, to visualize the person you would like to be, because it's easy to idolize characteristics that can never be you. Having a cool car, succeeding at sports, winning the class election, earning lots of money, getting good grades—boy, if you could do these things you would be a wonderful person, the person you want to be. Not so! These things do not make *you* and may not even go well with a you who is still floundering around, unsure of who you are. All right then. I'll be friendly to everyone, study hard, groom myself nicely, keep a cheerful attitude, treat my family well, imitate Christ in everything; then I'll be my ideal, the person I want to be. No. These are all good goals, but to attain them you would have to be either super-human or a phoney. Being you is much more simple and much more of a mystery than stacking up a lot of good qualities.

Becoming you is establishing very basic ideals, very basic responses which will serve you in your contact with life. When you are really alive, "with it," life's every experience is a confrontation with the opportunities of living in a wild, wide, growing world.

Brushing your teeth in the morning, dropping your books at the bus stop, getting the right answers in algebra, inviting a new girl to join your group for lunch, exploding at your little brother, asking the girl down the street to the prom, helping around the house, reading a good book, working things out with your folks; each of these things is a step in the formation of the real you. That's why all these actions often loom larger in your mind and emotions when they happen than they do later when you can put them in a larger framework.

Tension, conflict, embarrassment, chagrin; each is a test to see if the real you is prepared to take a step forward. You won't always emerge from crises as the more successful, more loveable person; but if you are striving to be the person who you know you must be, you will emerge each time a more confident and more secure person.

You won't become the permanent you this week, this month, or even this year. Still, you must begin becoming you today, and one bright morning a few hard years from now you will discover that *you know who you are* and *where you are going*. You will be predictable and acceptable; being yourself will be a fairly clear matter and, having arrived, you will like yourself. Don't be too surprised; don't wonder why you weren't aware of all this sooner, because the end is only reaping the fruit of the struggle taking place right now.

When you are least sure of yourself, when you are least prepared to face it, life comes tumbling toward you. No one understands you, nor do you understand yourself. It seems half the time you are embarrassed, hurt or in trouble. The balance of the time you are on cloud 9 and about to land with a thump. Rarely do things roll along smoothly. No advice will help you to make it turn out differently. The girl in your history class who seems to have all the answers can't tell you either. Chances are she is as bewildered about herself as you are; and by the way, your bewilderment doesn't show on the outside any more than hers does.

Being yourself means changing a little every day. It involves a lot of hammering and tempering in the process of shaping the complete you. Sometimes it is difficult because you are so unsure; the only guideline to follow then is BE. Keep being, keep living, keep loving, keep growing, keep changing. Do it gladly with gusto, for in teen-age to be yourself is to participate fully in the struggle to become yourself.

When you are still on the way, you are not yet someone; you are busy becoming a whole person, a "glued together" person. When, finally, you know yourself well, accept and love yourself completely, you will have arrived. You will no longer wear the tag "'teen"— you will BE; you will have given your name a person to stand behind it.

2

FISH--OR CUT BAIT

Tina Cole

How do we decide between beat and bossa nova? Should we dig folk-rock and crave the New Politics? I suppose our answers to these and similar questions will circumscribe and indicate our values. They will somehow guide us into the lives we ourselves set out to follow. They dictate our attitudes toward others we know and meet, causing Louis Evely to remark:

> "Loving people means summoning them forth
>   with the loudest and most insistent of calls;
> It means stirring up in them
>   a mute and hidden being
>   who can't help leaping at
>   the sound of our voice . . ."
>   *(That Man is You)*

We can say that the values which we have adopted, or which have been adopted for us, are the appropriate relationship which we have toward persons or things. These values appear to be person-oriented; individuals establish a value scale which operates for

5

them and them alone. "Her basic values are extremely stable" is a nicely constructed sentence, but what is it saying? Is she placing money above pickles because money is more secure as a means of exchange, or does she give uncompromising support to her values? Are we sure of what she means or does?

The most significant phrase of my definition is *appropriate relationship*. In my relationship with a priest I may place the highest value on his priestliness, or if he is also a professor, I may place greater value on his intellectual ability. If he is a personal friend, my orientation toward him would vary again. Most likely, I would place the greatest value on the sharing and loving we exchange through our common admiration.

In each instance I have entered into a distinct relationship with another person. My reaction to the person involved in this relation depends on the value I place on the role he encompasses. As a priest I may relate only to the man as distant or aloof. As a friend I relate more openly. At this point the appropriateness of any relationship must be considered.

My relationship with a priest-friend is centered on a growing together of two people who are free and comfortable, each in the other's presence, and who have a mutual trust. It would be inappropriate if I relate to my priest-friend as I relate to my boyfriend. With a boyfriend I naturally share myself in a more overtly loving manner. If I walked into the reception room of Father's home and we kissed affectionately, surely you would be taken aback, because we are not fulfilling our proper parts—we have transgressed our roles and are relating to each other in a most inappropriate manner. We have violated our friendship since we have placed the most value on an aspect of our relationship which is, according to our own hierarchy of values, inappropriate.

This is an extraordinary example, and as such makes it easier for us to visualize the way we develop our own values. It is thought-provoking and as such leads us into deeper discussion. The ideal situation places value on a person in his totality, neglecting nothing of which that person is made. Each person is irreplaceable and a center unto himself. External appearances are of no import in our evaluation of an individual, since it is the person himself we are discovering—the real person under the mini-dress. Each of us is a magnetic, dynamic person—a center, drawing others to us. We are totally open to the other, giving of ourself with no restrictions or conditions. We place value on people's openness. We value that which attracts us to their center—their real self. So we say.

But what about boys that neglect the personhood of a girl and relate only to her "beautiful bod?" Sure, a well-constructed body is beautiful to behold, but what of the person who expresses herself through and in her body? And what of the girls who, having the beautiful bods, dress to show them off? Are they not placing primary value on their outside curves and neglecting the warmth and personality of their inner self which has the most power to draw others to their "center?" I'm sure you know couples, who, going to the drive-in on their first date spend the entire evening making out, saying "I love you" and madly caressing each other. When Monday comes, they don't even remember each other's last name. If each person is a valued, irreplaceable individual, how can we defy his irreplaceability by making him replaceable? If you can make out on Friday with a chick and not know her name by Monday, you are saying she is not irreplaceable to me—her kisses and carresses are what I relate to and value, not her person. You are relating to her as a thing or a toy to be used, not as a person to be discovered.

Each of us is continually growing or becoming; if we stop and stagnate, we slowly die. As growing persons our individuality is continually asserting itself. Our growing personhood expresses itself actively in our relations with others and in our judgments about these relationships. As we stop to think about it, we realize that we place value on John's friendship because John has a mustang and willingly chauffeurs us about town; or we value dates with Susie because she is willing to play around. Conversely, we value a strong love-relationship with our parents because, after all, they did give us the best years of their lives.

The values with which we go sailing into adulthood were imbedded in our thoughts and acts from childhood. Why shouldn't we accept the value patterns of those about us—our parents, friends and peers—when we are young? As we mature, do we realize that "our" values are quite honestly those of our parents? Do we bother to try and decipher what we actually believe to be valuable in life, or do we merely continue to accept the values of others as we did in childhood? Our ability to examine our personal values and to accept them totally marks us as mature people.

This does not necessarily mean a renovation of our modes of thought or conduct. It involves a truthful and continuing evaluation of our personal philosophy. What, honestly, do we consider necessary to lead a good life? Are some values absolute? Deep inside, where only we can feel, what do we believe?

Our judgments must be considered in the context of relationships for it is with others that we become persons ourselves and truly realize what we consider to be of worth. For some, having a closetful of dresses or a car is living, or having a sailboat, or travelling or having a job. We should each try to recognize what we have that is valuably ours. I'm from a mixed-up, crazy, fun-loving large family. We encompass a range of ages and variety of interests. Yet each evening we sit down to a family meal and discuss—anything. I brought a friend, whom I wanted desperately to impress, home to dinner. The family ate together as usual, having a chit-chatty conversation when my younger sister started talking about her science class. Suddenly we were discussing the sex life of earthworms! I could gladly have disappeared—of all the things to discuss at dinner! On the way back to school my friend told me he enjoyed the entire evening. He thought it was great to see a family gathered together sharing ideas and adventures. His family seldom carried on anything but "proper" conversation at dinner and to him I was fortunate to have a sharing family. At that moment I doubted his judgment, but later I realized that my family is fortunate in an area where so many families are deprived.

Underneath all that, there was the basic stuff, the real significance of family life. I had placed value on the way my family would look and behave at the dinner-table and if he would pass approval. But his values of a real family unit were much more realistic and mature. I have come to realize that what you have is wonderful and even though I may be envious of another, I realize I have something of my own which I would never trade for goods—or ideas—or rights. I will rejoice at the good fortune of others, but shall always acknowledge my own good fortunes.

Developing values and judging their worth is one

thing. Living by our values, having strength of character to direct our lives in accordance with our values is another. We have the values and the intent—but do we have the courage to stand up, or even live what we believe? I am basing my entire value system and its continued development on the importance of each single life and my importance as a center drawing these individuals to me that I may love them unconditionally. I believe in love as the basic value, for from it flows all other values, desires and gifts. I consider love the core of all growth and life.

> "To love someone is to bid him to live,
>   invite him to grow.
> Since people don't have courage to mature
>   unless someone has faith in them,
> we have to reach those we meet
>   at the level where they stopped developing
> where they were given up as hopeless
>   and so withdrew into themselves
>   and began to secrete a protective shell
>   because they thought they were alone
>   and no one cared.
> They have to feel they're loved very deeply
>   and very boldly
> Before they dare appear humble and kind,
>   affectionate, sincere and vulnerable."

In this quote from *That Man Is You*, Louis Evely supplies the ultimate in value orientation. Can we be the men and women who are willing to be "That Man," to be vulnerable and open, placing ultimate value on the human centers around us?

HORTICULTURE FOREVER

Ivy continually entangles me
As it grows up
Around my body,
The calling of reason
Isn't from my ears,
And the Ivy grows
Around my body.

My friends call to me
And ask me to look.
See the sun,
The grass,
The lake vividly reflects
And the Ivy climbs around my body.

If the birds come to sing
I kick and I scream
For no one wants to be bothered.
Please leave me alone,
I know who I am
And the Ivy tightens
Around my body.

Some know that the earth
Holds riches untold,
But I know the things
that we find:
They're sterile and cold
And the Ivy entangles
My legs.

Leave me alone
For don't you know
No one knows a
Purpose for living.
I have all I need and am quite alive
And my chest can't move 'neath the Ivy.

My beauty is great,
I control all there is.
Unlike the statues that crumble,
Ages from now
I will still be.
And the Ivy stiffly
Bandages my throat.

Look says the Mass,
and I know
It is I they approach.
See his Beauty, see his strength.
My secret they want to know.
It is my Ivy so green,
New strength and my beauty.
To tell all the peasants.

Now is my time
To tell to these peasants
What makes me much better than they.
They laugh and they scorn
For they saw what I missed
And this Ivy?
Killed me before I was born.

Chris Lucey

3

SORRY ABOUT YOUR GOD

Rev. James L. Anderson

"God is dead!"

"God is everywhere!" But which is it? Who's right?

I thought the dull, "lifeless" memorization of religion was a thing of the past, long dead. To my surprise in the Fall of 1967 A.D. I received a note from a young friend in a Catholic school, run by a religious order credited with being "progressive." The note was written on the reverse side of a dittoed sheet from a religion class. There were the same questions and answers I memorized about forty years ago! "Where is God? God is everywhere." "If God is everywhere, why don't we see Him? We do not see God because He is a spirit and cannot be seen with bodily eyes."

Let's start from that point—I think it may lead us to some of the reasons why it seems that God is dead.

Maybe you were taught about God in this very same brief, question and answer form. I was taught my religion in this manner. I am not saying this "brief and to the point" technique did no good. Despite its limitations, it helped many to sink their roots deep in the good soil of faith. Every word is true. But, like most condensations, the tremendous concepts our teachers were trying to describe and explain were terribly limited and, worse, *limiting!* What do I mean "limiting?" I think that when we learned merely that God is "pure spirit" and "cannot be seen with bodily eyes" stated this way, these words tended to close the windows and doors and turned too many of us off as far as our human search for God is concerned. "He's pure spirit—He cannot be seen merely with human eyes."

In time, some of us were blessed to be awakened to look for Him and find Him. Too many others were not moved to look for Him and I think these are just some of the people who think He is dead.

They say that when one teaches, he learns from his students. This is true. While teaching high school and counselling, my relationship to my students moved me to search further for God. My obligations to them demanded I read and look for Him intellectually. Together, on a give and take basis, we found manifestations of his mighty power in the pounding surf at the beach. We were at his mercy riding a wave. His power surrounded us. We watched. We listened. We dreamed. We shared thoughts and we learned so much more there at the beach than in the classroom. Sadly, one cannot spend all his life and learn all life's lessons at the beach. Scaling steep mountains helped us in the same way. Again, one does not have to flee from the noise and confusion of the city to the luxurious quiet of the country to find Him. We thought, we shared and we learned lessons for a lifetime right in the city. The smooth-running traffic of the freeways and expressways reminded us that to the degree we observe His law of love and respect for others we find smooth order, love, happiness and respect in our own lives, be we realtors, bus-boys, politicians, mechanics, secretaries or what have you? The snarled traffic can teach the opposite— forget love and respect and—CONFUSION! The screaming sirens reminded us to think of the needs and problems of others. Maybe all we can offer is a prayer from the heart for them. That's a good start! The belching noon-day whistles remind us to take a few seconds or a minute or two to communicate with Him, even in the form of a good noisy, distractful dialog.

Everyone, and especially the wonderfully imaginative teenager, can train himself to seek out and find the ever-present God right in the city. We need but to open our eyes and ears and give our heads a whirl. Don't permit the catechism or anyone to limit your dreams for Him and your search for Him. I know—we have been frightened and therefore terribly limited in our search for Him in the past—fears of heresy and what not. He is everywhere, He is without limit— dream, dream, *dream!* Help all of us to find Him more and help all of us to learn more about Him. Beauty, power, love, kindness—they are all there and He is there—without limit.

A famous philosopher-scientist, Teilhard de Chardin, had much to do with clarifying for me a reasonable concept of God, one which puts a perspective on history and future, and relates the present to both. A few highlights of his writings indicate he was speaking to you and me when he offered the following suggestions:

1. In His unique manner of creating, God makes only *one you* with a special job to do, at a certain time in history, in certain environments. He has endowed you with very special talents. Take time to discover

these for yourself. Giving yourself to a job or a cause on a basis of the selfish acquisition of power, prestige, money and material things can prove disastrous both for you and for the world. Look around you today to find the destroying effects of such folly. You may already be tired of pressure "to make something of yourself" when it means "learn to make lots of money so you can hoard and hoard—so you can be rich and powerful." But what about self-fulfillment, the need of the world and you and happiness?

2. Do not disdain or lightly dismiss the past. You must study it well to discover the connecting fibers of truth which will help you to do your part to continue to weave the fabric of God's over-all plan. As much as we might like to think so, the world is not just starting with us!

3. Moved by the powerful "energies" of God's love, you must respond to it or die and be wasted. You must respond to God's love by giving yourself to Him by means of the gift of yourself to people and to the world. Your response to love will be in the form of the sacrifices you make to give people and the world the direction they need when they need it. You must care enough to give something of yourself.

Teilhard obviously takes a person way beyond the elementary paths to God such as I described at the beginning. One important elementary thought must never be forgotten—God is all around you. He is in you. He is in others. You must look for Him and must listen to Him. Do not be surprised; He will speak to you about the needs of people and of the world through countless varieties of media. Listen to Him as He alerts you to the needs of people and the world through the newscaster, the newspaper and TV. Discover people's joys and sorrows, well-being and confusion in the movies. This is life! Where and how are you needed? Listen to the bitter cries of frustrated Negroes and other minorities. Break out of the security of middle-class religion and dare to respect and listen to the message which movements, like the genuine hippies, are trying to put over—"we're tired of power and money pressure. Let's respect people as people. We're tired of hate and war and killing—let's try to love more. We're tired of hoarding talents and money and material things —let's try more to imitate the spirit of St. Francis."

Could it be that God is dead to the poor and suffering because He is dead in us? He is dead to the degree that our supermarket, Sunday-bargain-package Christianity did not go beyond sterile liturgical routine to fulfill an obligation.

We need to go to the rebellious, the bitter, the fallen, the messed-up, those we abandoned. They have a message for us and we can give a bit of meaning to their lives; all a part of the continuation of creation and redemption. This is contributing our part to the development of God's over-all plan. This is response. This is demonstration that God can be and is alive everywhere!

Now you think, "alone I can do little of this work—the pressures against me are too great." You are partially correct, partially incorrect. Do not underestimate yourself and what God can do through your witness. You are a social being and need to live and grow with others. You need to share ideas, joys, frustrations, companionship, inspiration; to keep trying despite disappointment and ridicule. You can be more effective united with others who have the same ideals and goals.

The following observations are the result of my association, working in groups, with young people. I hope that, after what I have said, no one will regard these ideas as "another imposition from the adult world." This doesn't mean, though, they shouldn't be aired and weighed by our thinking youth.

17

Everyone needs togetherness, the natural grouping of people with common interests. Youth should decide when a group has sufficient in common to act together. Growth comes about through the give and take processes of "association" with others. Let us call it community. There should be a minimum of organization and a lot of flexibility and adaptability when we work in groups.

Acceptance should be another characteristic of our group. God acts through all kinds of people and it is important to remember this if we are to reach realistic and objective conclusions. We do not like to put up with the person who demands reasons for things, we do not like the "troublemaker." But everyone has a contribution to make; we call these contributions "charisms." We must grow together in a spirit of openness.

Our group will grow through knowing and meeting the needs of the present and bringing God to those who need Him. We need creativity; but creativity will not grow in the midst of mistrust. We need to trust people enough to let them make mistakes. Without trust and allowance for mistakes, personal growth and world action will be very limited.

Our meetings should be a coming-together, needed by these people to share, evaluate, inspire, solicit the help of others and to celebrate. Where will plans for action come from? They will arise from the respective environments of the group members; their homes, schools, recreation, business, civic community, country and world community, as it comes to these people. Emphasis will be on the human person; the plan will be action needed to bring order out of chaos, love replacing hate and hurt, respect replacing disrespect. The process will involve setting up two-way streets for love and its response. We will need to be big enough to give ife and love and, sometimes more difficult, we will need to be big enough to accept love.

Where is God? Where there is LOVE, there is God. God is very much alive. He can be seen more obviously everywhere, but first, we need to look for Him and find Him ourselves. We must develop a life-long alertness.

God never tires of entrusting—notice, en-trusting, big jobs to little people like you and me. In reality, He's put the whole world in our hands. What it will be like depends on what people like you and me will do with it. Rejoice! Our God is alive!

4

SEX IS FOR REAL!

Dr. Joseph and Lois Bird

Many words have been written about sex; perhaps too many, or maybe too few. Philosophers have probed its meaning. Poets have rhapsodized its emotions. Theologians have wrestled with its morality, and physiologists have studied its biological aspects. Serious scholars have given us many valuable insights, and each year we still learn more. Despite these contributions, there is, even today, probably more misunderstanding and misinformation existent in the area of sex than in any other important area of human existence.

This is understandable if we remember that it has been only very recently that we have had any empirical study, anything which might properly pass as research, in the area of human sexuality. Even the most basic physiology of sex has been pretty much unknown until very recently. We know the reason for this. Always in the past sex has been buried in a taboo—not to be written about, not to be discussed and not to be investigated in a clinical fashion.

Fortunately, this has been changing, although we

have yet only scratched the surface in our search for knowledge. It is now only little more than a half century since Sigmund Freud, the father of psychoanalysis, opened the first doors and windows to admit some light on the subject. Since then there have been other men working in this area but, like Freud, they have encountered resistance and censure; they have met with hostility, rejection and a fear-motivated intolerance from a society which all too often has preferred the security of ignorance. Fortunately for us these men were willing to go forward. Now we have had an expansion of this research to the point where we can say we have truly empirical data in the form of large scale studies. Kinsey and his associates and, recently, Masters and Johnson have perhaps shed more light on the subject than had all previous writings combined.

We still have a long way to go, and we can expect to meet resistance. Many people still wish to see open discussion and candid writing on sexuality suppressed. Still others suffer from doubts and fears rooted in ignorance and ill-founded scruples. Those of us who are parents of teenagers grew up in an age of ignorance and we may still carry the aftereffects with us.

When we were children sex education was not taught in the schools. Then many people felt it was not a proper subject for the classroom, and even today some still oppose it. Books on Christian marriage during those years were simply awful. They paid, at best, only lip service to the notion that marital sexuality was good and holy. And yet, most of them gave the impression that in spite of what they wrote, sex was something unsavory. Because of this, many of us grew up with the vague idea that celibacy was the only "pure and holy" state, and that sexual relations were tolerated by God only so that the human race might be continued. All in all, the prevalent attitudes were pretty sick!

Our parents may have spoken to us of sexual love but all too often they suffered from the same unhealthy attitudes. If they told us anything, it was seldom more than the most sketchy biological facts, a sort of "birds and the bees" lecture on "where babies come from."

You have grown up in a far different environment. We sometimes wonder if you realize just how different. Now, sex has been brought out into the open. It has been liberated. Or should we say, you have been liberated, freed from the scruples, unhealthy attitudes and fears which plagued our generation. But is this true? Yes and no. And perhaps more no than yes. True, most of you, and even some of your parents, speak more openly of sex; and you are better informed than we were at your age. But there are still large gaps in both information and understanding of sex by both generations. Furthermore, those who have brought sex out in the open arena of the cocktail party and the high school campus have frequently failed to place sex in a suitable context. Love has been ignored; we have even changed its meaning to something very far from loving. And, in our rush toward sexual candor, we have somehow managed to lose sight of what it is we are talking about. We speak about sex, but seldom define it. There are people who claim our society is obsessed with sex, but they don't define it either. We happen to think they are confused. If there exists anything of an obsession, it is with an immature genitalism—but it isn't sex!

When we speak of human sexuality there is a relationship implied. In virtually none of the popular forms in which so-called "sex appeal" is employed—topless dancers, nude pin-ups, movie "sex goddesses"— can we find even the suggestion of a relationship.

The obsession—if we wish to call it by that name —has elements of voyeurism, exhibitionism, and even narcissism. But this is not sexuality, not the intimate relationship of a man and a woman. In fact, if it is pursued to its ultimate irrationality, men and women become only objects wholly unrecognizable as human beings. We find it interesting to ponder the fact that one of the more successful commercial exploitations of female sex symbolism has the semi-nude model dressed as a rabbit!

Many books and articles on sex are equally de-humanizing. They reduce sexual relations to a mere matter of technique and/or they write of love as solely a state of uncontrolled emotion, momentary and cha-otic. The emphasis is egocentric, and it is infantile; but it is more than prevalent.

By the sheer weight of these writings, and their dramatization through television and motion picture, love has become, for many, a dirty word.

How to account for this growing tendency toward becoming robots through a "new morality?" Have we really been freed of the "scruples, unhealthy attitudes, and fears" of previous generations? We don't think so. It seems more probably that we still have the same old hang-ups, and they are as strong as ever. We have now, however, put them in a new dress. If we can reduce sex to mere biologism—physical acts with little or no psy-chological import and no spiritual meaning—we can successfully, perhaps, defend against an anxiety which is not so much a fear of a physical act as it is a fear of a human relationship—with emphasis on the word "human."

When we uncover the roots of the problem, we discover this has always been the inhibiting, sometimes crippling fear, one which has touched us all. We all fear exposing ourselves, showing our emotions. It is a feeling of vulnerability. Human sexual encounters, if they are to be other than mechanistic, call for a full mutual exposure of personalities, a "knowing" of each other. What we fear is revealing weakness; it would give our partner some piece of information to use against us. We fear ridicule and criticism, and this is hardly surprising. We have all, at one time or another in our lives, had our fingers burned because we exposed them. So if we talk about sex in a sort of detached impersonal way, we avoid any such self-exposure. But if we do this, we also miss really knowing another human being on what could be called a "meaningful" level. And, we even miss discovering some truths about ourselves.

It is in self-knowledge that we find the greatest gaps. We see little to suggest that most of the people doing the talking about sex have an understanding of their own sexuality, or their interpersonal relationships with both sexes.

We learn our sexual attitudes, healthy or unhealthy, and we seldom take them out and look at them. Instead, we tend to moralize them; we tack the label "right" or "wrong" on all things sexual, whether or not there is any moral issue involved. But, we may not stop to think about how we acquire these attitudes in the first place or whether or not they aid our growth and development as persons. A sound moral base is essential to mature sexuality, but such moralizing is detrimental to any growth.

We often think of sexual thoughts and feelings as reactions which begin at the onset of puberty. Some writers, at least by implication, even define puberty in these terms: "the period in one's life when sex begins." This is a mistake. Our "sex life" is part and parcel of our total life. It begins when we are conceived and it ends with our death. If we view it differently and hold, for example, that the sex life extends only from the early teens to the mid-fifties, we may fall into the trap of genitalism and a false splitting of "mind and body" or "spirit and flesh."

We don't acquire a sexual nature; we are born with it. Much as some modern writers would have us believe that society somehow turns us into men or women, the fact remains that society has not yet been able to change the sex of a single individual. Certainly we have effeminate males and masculine females, but regardless of mannerisms and behavior, they remain what they were born: male or female. No one is born neuter.

The first signs of what we can call the sexual drive show up in early infancy, even before we take our first steps, or utter our first words. We begin developing relationships with other human beings, physical relationships, touching, being held, receiving (although not yet giving) physical affection. And it is pleasurable. Is it also sexual? Yes, if we broaden our definition of "sexual" a bit, because in these early relationships we are aided in developing an awareness of our bodily sensations. Also, we gradually learn sexual distinction; the difference between male (Daddy) and female (Mommy).

We also become aware of bodily sensations and their pleasure, through self-discovery, the exploration of our own bodies. We bring our fingers to our mouth and discover the pleasure of thumb-sucking. We investigate our fingers, our toes, and our genitals. And we find that touching and stimulating our genitals is pleasurable.

This is upsetting to many parents, and they search for ways of preventing self-stimulation. Their fears are, however, groundless and their means of prevention can be seriously harmful to the child. Suppressive measures communicate unhealthy sexual attitudes. They teach the child to view the body as "bad" and bodily sensations as "wrong."

Other attitudes are similarly communicated. These attitudes take shape long before the child reaches puberty, most of them, in fact, before the child enters kindergarten. They are formed in a reflection of the parents' attitudes and are communicated on largely a nonverbal level. The look of disgust when the three-year old parades through the living room sans clothes, the embarrassment when he asks one of "those questions" or, worst of all, the punitive action taken when the child is caught doing something "naughty," will do much to shape unhealthy attitudes. Mom and Dad may not discuss sex with the child, but they will communicate sexual attitudes even in their silence (perhaps that sex is "unspeakable"). They will also teach attitudes through what they are as a man and woman, husband and wife. Whether they intend it or not, they will reveal their marriage. Perhaps in this way, more than by any other means, the child will form sexual attitudes through observing that marriage. Attitudes toward the opposite sex, toward marriage, toward God, and toward oneself will also be shaped in this parental image and the picture of the parent's marriage. The parents may never fight in front of the children, but the children will perceive a strained relationship if it exists. Mother may say that sex is "good and holy," but if she personally found little meaning and satisfaction in the marital union, she will pass on only negative feelings.

As we progress toward adolescence, we encounter other influences: teachers, friends, priests and nuns, and the ever-present mass media. All may contribute to the formation of our attitudes and reactions. Not all will be positive influences. Perhaps most of them will be otherwise. We simply do not live in a world which reflects the best views of what we are and what we can become as men and women.

What then if we have been subjected to a large dose of unhealthiness? Are we destined to carry unwholesome sexual attitudes? Not by any means. An influence is just that: an influence. It may be positive or negative, weak or strong, but it need not stamp us for life. We can root out the negative attitudes we have been taught; we can reject them and replace them with an ideal and a mature acceptance of self. If may not be at all easy, however. Accepting the presence of unwholesome attitudes in ourselves can be disturbing; recognizing that these attitudes came from those closest to us can be intensely painful. The process is not a little like surgery. But surgery is imperative at times.

By the time we have physically matured to the point where our bodies are prepared for adult sexual behavior, we have progressed a great distance. Nevertheless, puberty does strike with a suddenness. It does seem like the beginning of something very new; and it is. Very rapid changes take place throughout the entire body. It is as if all of a sudden our endocrine glands wake up and start functioning at top speed. Soon, secondary sex characteristics appear. However, these changes in the figure, hair distribution, and voice are only the obvious. The whole body undergoes change. Girls begin to look—and act—very differently from boys; and boys begin to notice the difference.

Dramatic as these changes are, the psychological changes are even more profound. Unless the child has been taught to suppress all sexual feelings and thoughts to the extreme, new and exciting stimuli burst into consciousness, often with great force. The thoughts and feelings are equally strong in both sexes. At times, they seem to move in and take over all our thoughts. They can be disturbing and distracting, but if we accept them as we should, we find them one of the choicest gifts we, as human beings, have been given.

In our teens we may experience our first deeply emotional encounter with the opposite sex. These encounters can be very painful as well as very exciting. Being in love is fun, but it's no fun being rejected by the one you may have fallen for pretty hard. And it helps little or none at all for the well-meaning parent to say, "Forget it, it's only puppy love." It can't be passed off that easily. The emotions may well be as intense, and the pain as deep, as any that will ever be felt. The pain which is felt during these years is all the more severe because the emotional defenses so available to the adult have not yet been fully developed. The adolescent is emotionally wide open.

There are other pains in adolescence. All in all, it is a period of unrest and loneliness, rejection and rebellion. Those adults who speak of the teens as years of carefree joy must somehow have reached adulthood without passing through adolescence or else their experience was truly unique. It may be possible that they have just forgotten. Sure, there may be a lot of fun, but the teens also have more than a share of heartache and conflict. Many adjustments are demanded, social situations and involvements change rapidly. Not all of us, of course, experience the same conflicts, nor to the same degree of intensity, but two areas of conflict touch nearly every adolescent: parents and sex—and the ways in which we cope with both. What is more, the conflicts often bear on one another.

The conflict with parents is often not so much a conflict between parent and child, although these "family battles," as we all know, can be fierce and frustrating, as it is an internal conflict for the teenager, one of autonomy vs. dependence.

During the first dozen or so years of life we are almost totally dependent on adults. We view our parents as godlike. They seem to have all the answers and can do anything and everything. We need to see them in this way; it provides security. As we enter adolescence, however, we no longer feel this strong need for dependence. If we have matured as we should, we will at this point begin to venture out into the world in which we live, to shape our role in it, and free ourselves of parental direction and control. This is normal, a healthy sign of growth. If we make no attempt to try our wings at this age, we may end up emotional cripples later on in life.

This growth does give rise to conflicts, with our parents and with our own conflicting needs. We desire independence, the right to decide "on our own." We want recognition as an adult—or at least as a person no longer a child. At the same time, there is a comfort found in remaining dependent, the security of childhood. It is tempting to avoid the responsibilities of adulthood. In adolescence, we often vacillate between the two, at times independent and responsible, at other times childishly irresponsible and demanding. Still more frequently, we try to claim the "best of both worlds"—demanding the rights of independence, while at the same time claiming the advantages of dependence on parents. Haven't we all listened to our parents say something like, "You want us to treat you as an adult, but you won't assume your responsibilities!"

There is, we must all admit, some validity in the

words, but in many cases they also reveal an insecurity common to parents, as well as habits built up over the period of child-rearing. Parents have many years of practice in making the responses expected of parents, and these habits don't give way overnight. Is there some magical age at which the young person should suddenly appear fully mature, some obvious event which should signify adulthood and change the relationship of parent and child? The answer is obvious. It is a gradual transition. On the sixteenth birthday one doesn't appear much different or more mature than the day before; and the same can be said of the twenty-first or the thirtieth. We grow up, but parents don't stop being parents any more than children cease being their children.

We, the parents, are often unaware that we are treating our children as younger than they actually are. We don't intend to, perhaps, but our anxieties get in the way. The thought of their children being out on their own in a hostile world can scare the calmest parents. We may recall our own mistakes and the senseless follies of our youth, the wasted opportunities, the purposeless risks and we try, by advice and admonition, to protect our children. We worry and fuss over their school performance, their driving, the hours they keep, their diet and the friends they select.

We may not admit it even to ourselves, but just under the surface of many of our concerns is the awareness that our teenage son or daughter is sexually an adult, with all the sexual drive and feeling of an adult. To some parents, this is an unseen, frightening enemy, a force threatening the moral and emotional life of the child. They react in an almost paranoid fashion with suppressive measures and unjust accusations.

The adolescent doesn't have to be told of these feelings. They are very real and very present. Nor does he or she need to be told that sex lies at the base of some of these conflicts with parents. It crops up in the questions of dating—where, with whom and doing what. It plays a part in arguments over "proper" or "improper" dress, questions of going steady, and wrangles over curfew hours. It may be stretching it to say sex underlies all of these, but it does account for very much. It is the fear of sexual involvements, coupled with a concern for reputation, which motivates parents to set what may be unreasonable limits.

What can be said of this situation? The teenager argues that the parents don't trust him, and they don't understand, that they're old-fashioned. He may be right, at least partially. These are areas in which communication frequently fails, and pretty miserably so. It fails because both parties, the parent and child, play a deceptive and destructive game, one which goes something like this. The parents want to see their teenagers as very naive, almost to the extent of not knowing the basic "facts of life." We have actually heard a parent say, "Our son doesn't know what sex is all about; after all, he's only sixteen." Well, he may be a child in some respects, but he isn't mentally retarded, nor has he been raised in a monastic cell!

The teenager plays the role expected of him: he plays dumb. When speaking with their parents, adolescents pretend to be much more ignorant of sex than they are. For this reason not much of anything is ever said about sex, at least nothing candid.

The game offers comfortable rewards for both parent and child. For the parent, so long as the belief in the child's ignorance can be sustained, there is little fear of sexual experimentation. And for the teenager, so long as he or she can play the game of being ignorant and innocent, his parents may not be quite so prone to set stringent limits. Dad and Mom may be quicker to give permission to stay out late at the movie if they never suspect their daughter of leaving the movie early to park somewhere with her boyfriend.

Teachers also often have the same "wool-over-the-eyes" picture of teenage reality. We have heard talks on marriage and sex given by high school and CCD teachers which might have been appropriate for twelve-year-olds given to high school seniors. When we asked one group of students why they didn't speak out and let the teacher know, the answer came from a sixteen-year-old girl: "So long as she wants to see us as ten-year-olds, why burst her bubble?"

Perhaps someone should burst the bubble. The truth of the matter is that sex is today freely discussed among adolescents and many of them are more experienced in sexual areas than even the most sophisticated parents suspect. Yet so long as the game of "we don't know what it's all about" is played, the truly important issues and questions are never confronted. If, on the other hand, the facades are stripped away and both parents and adolescents attempt to be frank, lines of communication can be developed which will aid personal sexual growth—perhaps for everyone concerned.

Many of you in your teens view sex quite differently than did your parents' generation. In some respects your views may be more healthy. Only you, in your own experiences, will be able to judge; but you are going to have to be very honest. You are going to have to ask yourselves questions, lots of them, and be willing to search long and hard for the answers. No one, not your friends, not your parents, not even your church, can hand you any answers on a platter. If you do close your eyes and settle for half-truths and distortions, you will, in time, pay the price in unhappiness.

II

As a beginning, one might examine the rather artificial tri-part way we talk about sex and sexual morality: thoughts, words and actions.

Most of what has been written about the morality of sexual thoughts—those ideas and daydreams which are sexually stimulating—has been sheer nonsense. It has lacked any concise definitions and has been written from an appalling ignorance of human psychology. There are people who teach, at least by implication, that all sexual thoughts and desires are sinful. Granted, they may not come right out and say this in so many words, but this is the message they convey. Many of us in the "older" generation got a heavy dose of this doctrine. Any thought, however, and thinking is far too rare, applied to this question will lead to the conclusion that sexual desire, far from being sinful, is a basic part of our nature as human beings. To reach adolescence and not experience such thoughts and desires would be abnormal. They are just as much an indication of approaching adulthood as are the changes in our bodies. The two go hand-in-hand.

Other people say it isn't sexual thoughts and desires which are immoral, but the pleasure taken in them. This is equally absurd. If we don't find pleasure in sexual thoughts and desires, we probably need help. Of course they are pleasurable; they should be. And wasn't God good to us in giving us something which is so pleasurable? Without them we would be less than human.

Are there, then, no impure thoughts? No, not as we

see it, since we can find nothing impure in human sexuality, and isn't that what they are talking about as "impure?" Words, and the ways in which we employ them, help form our attitudes and they reflect the attitudes we hold. This is particularly true in the area of sex. We learn words like dirty, smutty, off-color and impure, and if we adopt them, whether or not we recognize it, they will reflect our attitudes. We may try to pass it off by saying it is only immoral sex which is dirty but then, why isn't stealing a dirty act and why don't we call a motion picture glorifying war a "dirty movie" and why don't we call an act of racial discrimination a "dirty act?" Yes, some sexual thoughts may lack beauty and love; they may be devoid of wholesomeness, humanity and godliness but this makes them only rather pathetic, not impure or dirty. We should think about sex and discuss it and attempt to understand it, and we should strive to understand and accept gratefully our feelings of sexual arousal and discard the guilt which comes from viewing these thoughts and feelings as sinful.

We can say the same of so-called "dirty" words. Some people seem to have the idea that there are certain words which, regardless of context, are in and of themselves immoral and that these words are, for some vague reason, sinful. If we stop to think, we can see that these views are conditioned emotional responses, nothing more. Words are words. If they best express what we hope to communicate, we should use them. We may, of course, find that some of the so-called four letter words are unacceptable to others and therefore, even though they may communicate we may choose not to use them; but it isn't in any case, a moral issue. Words are no dirtier than thoughts.

34

So much for thoughts and words. Now to the nitty-gritty: sexual actions.

With disturbing frequency we have listened to what we call "limits" questions. These are the kind which ask for a line to be drawn, a moral limit to be set. "How far can you go in making out?" "Is french kissing sinful?" "Is it permissible to do so and so?" They are asking, "Where do we draw the line?" as if morality is nothing other than a code of laws, a collection of "no-no's."

This isn't Christianity, and to view our moral obligations solely in terms of what we "shall not" do is to miss the whole point. Christ stressed what we must do if we are to share in His life, not what we must avoid doing. He told us to love. Love was to be the new law, the law of Christ (Gal 6:2)

We seem to have lost sight of this. What does it mean to us in an age in which we hear so much talk of love and so little loving; an age in which so many are so desperately, so neurotically, seeking to be loved, and so few are striving to love? An age in which very few can even adequately define love?

Let's try. To start with, love is not an emotion, and it is important that this be understood. Love is not some sort of feeling, nor some state into which we fall. Love is an act of will. It is the conscious choice of giving something of oneself to another. It is not something which happens to us, but a decision which we make, upon which we act.

An understanding of love is of such importance to our attainment of maturity and our growth in Christianity that we simply cannot overstress these points. We have asked, "Could you love someone you might never have met, someone of whom you knew little or nothing?" We are not talking about "love at first sight," that almost lightning sudden attraction for another. We are talking about love. What would your answer be? Would you say it would be impossible to love someone unless you knew them and found them attractive and "loveable?" Most people feel this way; but hold on a minute. We have all heard of some heroic man or woman risking his or her life, or even sacrificing it, to save the life of a stranger. Isn't this love? "Of course," many will answer, "but it's a different kind of love."

No, it isn't. Love is love. There are not different kinds and varieties. Any act in which you give of yourself for the good of another is an act of love. There are, to be sure, differing relationships and differing ways in which to love. The relationship of parent and child differs from that of husband and wife or brother and sister. They differ in emotional intensity and in the needs expressed and met, but these emotions, intense as they may be, are not love. We may have little conscious control over our emotions, but we can make our choices of loving. If love were the emotion, and pretty much beyond our control, we would be forced to conclude that Christ was unrealistic or unjust in demanding that we do something not within our control!

Are we saying then that we can love anyone we make up our mind to love? The answer is YES, but only if we are talking about love—mature love. There will be, of course, human limitations. I may want to save someone from drowning, but if I can't swim, I will not be able to do so. There are also limits imposed by our emotional growth. A child, or an adult who is still clinging to emotional childhood, cannot fully love. Loving —the choices of giving—is the act of a mature, responsible adult. One who gives his life for another, we call a hero. We might, instead, call him an adult, since an adult is one who lives a life which is a succession of heroic choices. These choices are seldom as dramatic as a life-saving rescue.

Any choice which is made without concern for self-interest, which is made out of desire to give to another, is heroic—and adult—and very much Christian. To the extent to which we are free to choose our actions, and this is to a far greater extent than most of us care to admit to ourselves, we can make loving choices.

Then where does emotion come into the picture, or do we just ignore our feelings? Of course not. We wouldn't want to even if we could, and we can't. Emotions are one of the characteristics which distinguish humans from other animals. Though they may be painful at times, they give us the awareness of being alive. Without them, we would be little more than zombies. There is something, however, which we often fail to recognize: by our actions we can influence and even control our emotions.

Perhaps the easiest way to understand this is to consider what happens emotionally to the mother of a newborn infant. At that time in its life the child can give nothing to the mother. It doesn't even respond to her. It doesn't say "thank you" or smile in appreciation. The baby is totally dependent on the parent. She feeds the child, bathes it, changes its diapers, rocks it to sleep, and performs all the other tasks necessary to the baby's comfort and well-being. She is willing to endure most anything, perhaps even death, for the sake of her child. We speak of it as "mother love." Mother love seems so universal that we tend to think of it as an instinct, but it isn't. There is nothing innate in the emotions a mother feels toward her baby. If the child came to her through adoption, she would not care less. Yet don't we hear some people claim that one can love only if they are loved in return?

In truth, it is in loving, not in being loved, that the deepest of positive emotions arise. One simply cannot give to another, consistently and without reservation, without experiencing the very deep emotion many people speak of as love. Certainly, as we all know, we can experience the emotional attraction without having given anything at all. In fact, this is usually what we speak of as "falling in love." If these feelings are to be more than off-again-on-again emotions, the acts of loving must follow, and they must increase and continue to grow. Alan Watts, the philosopher, put it rather well when he said, "Many claim the honeymoon ends when the young couple come up against reality, but that, in truth, the honeymoon ends when the couple kill reality—the only true reality: Loving."

To return now to the question of sexual actions. We have said we don't answer these "limits" questions. We don't even try. We do not believe that one person can provide answers for another. Our answers, if they are to provide meaning and direction, must be our own. They must be uncovered through our personal search, never through a rule book.

The answers can be found, but they will be found to have validity for us only if we ask, "What does Christ ask me to do?" rather than, "What does God forbid me to do?" In doing so we can build a personal ethic and a foundation in morality which is truly Christian. This does not, of course, in any way mean that one should ignore the counsel and insights of others. On the contrary, we can form a mature conscience only if we are informed, only if we look and listen, read, study and pray. This isn't always the easiest plan to follow. Sadly enough there are too few appropriate models in our society, too few who appear to have found meaningful answers in their own lives, but in any conclusive analysis we are going to discover Christ and learn what he is asking of us only through a personal encounter and a continual struggle toward an ideal.

If we hold to the ideal of loving, we may be able to find general answers which will provide a framework within which to answer the specific questions about sexual actions.

Sexual intercourse is often referred to as "love making." We like the words. It should be the making of love. Divorce the act from love and it is little more than an act of exploitation or mutual self-seeking; take away love and the act touches neither the human nor the divine. However, in order for the act to be truly love-making, it must be motivated by more than emotion or physical arousal; it must be a mature, and mutual, gift of self for the good of another. Psychologically, it is even more. Inherent in the act is a mutual commitment, a promise of selfless dedication. We may shut our eyes to the commitment; we may even deny it. We may attempt to rationalize our actions, but in doing so we stand to lose all we have been promised and all we have been called to become as brothers and sisters of Christ. This commitment can best be described as a promise to give one's life to that particular person. It is more than saying, "I love you." It is communicating by the most intimate of physical actions, "I love you and I promise to give you all that I am, to live my life for you, to proclaim to all the world that I am yours and you are mine." It is this implied pledge which makes the act of sexual love the most profound, the most deeply meaningful of all human actions. It is in this commitment, this promise of lasting unity that the physical union touches the divine union of the Trinity and becomes "a glimpse of the Beatific Vision."

This is an ideal, and we freely admit we are idealists. To some, this seems foolish; it just isn't practical, they will tell you. They scorn the idealism of youth, and view it as a mark of immaturity. It isn't. As a matter of fact one who is not an idealist and is not willing to cling to, and to defend, his ideals and convictions, can have little hope of attaining adulthood; that mature acceptance of responsibility which enables one to live heroically. If we accept and strengthen this ideal, any questions concerning what we should or should not do sexually with another can be answered not with the simplistic approach of searching for rules, but through an honest attempt to answer the question, "Is this truly loving; am I attempting to give something of myself for the good—physically, psychologically and spiritually—of this person?"

Only a fool would claim to have found easy or simple answers. Our sexuality is complex and the challenges are great. We know; we have faced them. Those days before we married are still vivid. We remember the conflicts, the questions, the doubts and fears, the guilt feelings, the successes, the failures, the loving and the lack of loving. Did we learn from it? We feel sure we did but what answers we found did not come from listening to the moralizing of those who emphasized sin rather than love. They did not come from concentrating on what we should not do, with one exception: we learned to avoid those who presented sex and marriage in the most cynical terms—and they always seemed to be in the majority.

We didn't have answers for the cynics then, only a dream. The cynics told us we couldn't expect the honeymoon to last; they said marriage was a matter of give and take, a kind of "putting up with one another" and they said sex would lessen in its importance; one couldn't expect it to retain its excitement. They said, "Wait until you've been married two years (or five, or seven); wait until you have three (or four, or six) children." Always they predicted doom—or dullness.

Now we can answer them. Now we have outlasted and outnumbered the cynics. The honeymoon hasn't ended; it has become even more a honeymoon. Every year our marriage has become more romantic, more exciting, more swinging, and in every respect more fun. It has become, in the fullest sense, our vocation, our sole vocation. Now we understand why it has been called "the sacrament of sexual love."

We have no sage bits of advice. We are not going to suggest that you stay out of parked cars, take along a chaperone, or practice some magical devotion designed to overcome temptations. We suggest only that you search, in prayer and honesty. What answers you will find will be your own; they must be. If they contribute to your personal growth and eventual happiness, they will be found through striving to understand yourself, seeking to know Christ, and endeavoring to love.

5

MARRiAGE--LOVE-iN FOR REAL

Gerald and Geraldine Raffo

From the vantage point of four years of married life we want to share with you the greatest adventure you can imagine—living together. Four years does not exactly qualify us as experts but since one of us is in that special and hallowed under-25 group and the other in that much-maligned over-30 group, we thought we'd at least present a perhaps more believable approach to marriage, combining both the traditional and evolving concepts about marriage. We hope you understand that we, too, are continually having to revise and renew our commitments to each other and to our children. We are in that group of middle liberals who are trying to understand the world you have been living in all your life, meld it with the world in which we grew up as youngsters and somehow effect a synthesis. It is very frustrating at times. We hope that after reading our ideas you will know better the essentials of marriage and be better able to cope with the evolving pattern of marriage. Your age group, with your demand for honesty, responsibility and freedom can take up the gauntlet which couples like ourselves are throwing out to you. The world can be changed and marriage is a vital way of life in accomplishing that change. We would like to discuss that beguiling and seductive motto of the psychedelic movement, "Turn on, Tune in, and Drop out." If you substitute spirituality for drugs, then this motto takes on meaning which can change your outlook today and lead you to the experience of a beautiful married life. So, let's start at the beginning.

THE "THREE" STATES OF LIFE

Let's face it. Very few in our generation believed that there were truly three callings in life. There were those in school who always seemed destined for the religious life. Some may have overacted the holiness bit; or maybe they told everyone they wanted to "go in," or maybe they were in that group who always surprised everyone with their decision. "How can such a pretty girl with all those boyfriends go off to the convent?" Or maybe, it was the team captain. Both these types were considered slightly odd. After all, how could they give up children, home and sex? It was hard to see anything but their supreme sacrifice as a call from God. Many of us who might have answered that call closed our mind to this way of life.

The second state was married life. Into this category fell, literally, almost everyone else. The third state of life comprised those people waiting to marry someone, or those who had missed the boat either out of duty toward family, or because no one wanted them. Only a very, very few actually chose the single state. Many of us thought the choice was black and white. We certainly didn't get the call, so it must mean that we are supposed to be married. Most of the time you don't really think about marriage as a state you choose to be in; of course you want to be in it. Right? So we tend to think of marriage as a life of love and sex, peaceful coexistence with children and above all security and status.

Attitudes are now changing. There are at present three distinct ways of life. Take a look at the religious life as it is evolving after Vatican II. Where can you find opportunity to develop your whole personality, with freedom from some of the household and emotional drudgery of marriage and where you can fulfill your dreams of social commitment, as greatly as you can as in some of the religious orders? All this, remember, within a religious family of adults. The religious life today no longer poses a threat to individuality; rather it is a challenge to serve in a special way—a life of adventure.

Look at the single life. There are ever increasing numbers of people forming lay institutes. They are well-adjusted people who have normal needs and desires, who feel that while religious life is not for them they still want to give their lives to God and to their communities. There are those among you who will go to the Peace Corps or Vista or into the myriad other social organizations and professions where single life will be fulfilling and very meaningful. You may stay unmarried and not feel unwanted or alone. Some married people you will know will not look smug and say "She isn't fulfilled or happy." They will realize this is the best possible life for you and that marriage, hopefully, was the best possible choice for them. There are those, too, whose careers would be impeded by marriage; some who feel that marriage is a great burden and those who feel this way, the life-long children, we hope, will have the courage not to marry. Indeed the single non-religious life is receiving a new acceptance and a new status in our marriage-minded society.

So what makes you feel you should be married? You can't decide by a process of easy elimination. You have to think about what marriage entails and what it is going to demand of you. Face it—you will live in the spirit of poverty, chastity and obedience, not free to do much of what you personally want. You may never be part of a great social involvement and you may run the risk of becoming a middle-class hypocrite. Why do people take this chance? There is no doubt that, with the religious and single lives presenting wonderful alternatives and with society warning of population explosions and soaring divorce rates, you have to know what life you are choosing. Falling in love with someone is not the criterion. Everyone can fall in love regardless of their state of life. The important thing is to know yourself and pray. If marriage really is your vocation and you want to be honest Christians in today's highly complex and materialistic society; if you want to better your parents at shaping the world; if you want to leave your mark, then marriage will be the most exciting and challenging life you can expect for yourself. We say this without reserve. If you want to marry and are prepared for it, then the life will not let you down.

THE LOVE-IN

Since the beginning of man's existence he has been involved in a love-in with all creation and with God. When a man marries, his very existence depends upon the love-in between God, his beloved and himself. Depending upon the honesty of this original love-in you can allow life to open up to include a limitless number of people. Marriage can be the most authentic love-in because you not only open all your physical senses to life and love and freedom but, integrated with them, you open up your spiritual senses. Thus with the totality of humanness, body and soul, you can, as man and wife, love God.

Usually in chapters such as this, the authors, if husband and wife, say they are deeply in love. We do love one another very much, as deeply as you can in a short three and one-half years. That marriage is like nothing you have ever experienced sounds a little too obvious to be meaningful, doesn't it? Each of you think dating is preparing you for actual married life. You might, as we did, think that dating gives you insights into the man-wife relationship, but it doesn't. It does provide a way of choosing someone you may love, a way of being with a variety of personalities, but it doesn't let you in on the exciting life of "two in one flesh" as St. Paul said, the life which makes a home.

When a "flower-child" offers you a flower or some beads, this is a token to you of the overflow of "being," of openness; perhaps you might term it love. You can accept or reject it, it doesn't effect their desire to give. If you do accept, you become vulnerable, for you may find that you want to give a part of yourself or of your philosophy in return. This may be painful. To accept, in the first place, involves a commitment to give something, just as the giving involved a commitment to love. When you begin your marriage you are so totally "in love" that you miss the responsibilities of love. For instance, never before have you encountered the necessity of blending two individual selves into a common unit. We think that those couples who have not found challenges in this area have not loved each other enough to meet their differences head on. It is a fantastic process which goes through the spectrum of mere trifles, such as what side of the bed to sleep on, to the nitty-gritty of spiritual and psychological change. Your wife or husband will want all of you—mind, body and spirit. It never ends. You don't go home to your family at night to be your old self again. This is the beginning of that process which sometimes ends in the almost extra-sensory perception which some couples seem to have.

At the start, and you may have found this out in dating, you seem to take on the entire personality of the other person. You may become a doormat. Many wives fall into this martyr role, never demanding anything from their husband, much less from their families. You may, however, guard your individuality fiercely and refuse to integrate yourself totally with your spouse. We have seen marriages where husband and wife are like friends cohabitating together. Essentially each goes off on his own way, whether it be a career, civic work or self-indulgence. Hopefully you will take the real plunge and forge out the married individual-you. In most cases you will end up a better person than the original you. This is when your marriage may surprise you because it is so rocky. After all, they say marriage ends all the inconveniences and quarrels that are a part of dating and courtship, or does it?

As far as we are concerned, when you marry, you marry your best friend, your confidant, and your lover. This person must be tops. We are against maintaining confidants, especially parents and best run-around pals outside of the two of you. You are a couple—a new unit, ready to make your history together. We hope you take this in the common-sense way in which it is intended and we know that you know what we mean. Too many problems arise when you confide your problems, arguments and husband-wife frustrations to anyone else but your spouse. Your spouse is your first line of communication in these matters and because of this mutual communication you will find your interest in each other growing constantly, day by day. You will never be bored by each other and you will be constantly amazed that your love affair is never over. You know that feeling as the flame of a romance burns out; you want to get out and fast and have nothing more to do with it. However, surrounded by the permanence of marriage and by the love-gifts of body and mind you always find something new and fresh out about each other. Remember that each individual is a limitless creature, so even if you are married fifty years you could never plumb fully the depths of each other. When you think about it realistically, you realize that your love will not always manifest itself in a sudden rush of excitement; though at times when we see each other it is there, it will not always come as a rush of pride and respect for the other; it may come in a quarrel or in the sometimes sheer monotony of marriage. This love comes imperceptibly in everything you do. It is not only your love, but God's love for you both. When things are at their best or worst, or quite calm, the graces of marriage which belong to you will come and work their change in you.

All of this involves before marriage a kind of emotional self-examination, a survey of your own hopes, desires and the acquisition of the skills of communication. This last—the acquisition of the skills of communication—is not only more necessary and practical than learning to cook or having a fabulous job, it is vital to married life.

To be candid, we can't skirt the issues about marriage which are causing so much controversy and frustration to both men and women today. These center largely around the emergence of women in competition with men in our society. Be honest, fellows, is the air of independence and self-sufficiency you treasure in your girl what you really want in your wife? Many of you, though you may not admit it, are traditionalists at heart and the ideal of a modern but definitely homespun girl is part of you. It is O.K. to date an aggressive or highly intellectual girl, but you wouldn't want to marry one. Right?—or wrong? Some of you might feel threatened by the changing status of the American female.

Do you want a girl that has been brought up with equal opportunity for the sexes, packaged foods and freedom to play the traditional role exclusively? If she did, she wouldn't do it forever; democracy is here to stay. Perhaps what you think St. Paul meant when he said: "Wives be subject to your husbands" is not at all how your wife will interpret it. Women have been fighting too long for equality and recognition to lose their status as adults when they marry. Thus, evaluating what real masculinity is and what a true head of the household is are essential for your security in marriage and peace of mind for both of you. Don't be fooled. Wives all need a Rock of Gibralter, just as men need a loving haven. It is the accidentals that are changing, not the essentials. All this change is for the better. By being her fullest self in you, you will, in turn, find yourself through her. You will find her a receptive, intelligent listener and a true help-mate.

It seems we have let the girls off the hook. Not so. With your new status comes additional responsibilities. When the chips are down you will most likely still wash the traditional dishes, or at least fill the dishwasher most of the time. You cannot put the ideal of personal fulfillment over the needs of your husband and your family. You must come to a working arrangement so you are not stifled. It takes a lot of soulsearching to achieve the balance that is best for you and your family. If a dirty floor drives you into a tizzy, then you have to budget the time to get it done. If it doesn't, you probably won't mind waiting an extra day or two to get it clean. It is up to you and to your husband.

What do you think you will want from a husband? Have you ever thought seriously about it? Will you expect him to help you in the house? Will he do the things that your father does and that you think all men do in their own homes? Have you found yourself playing a role with each different date? Are you prepared to run a house and care for a family and still have time to cultivate your own personal interests? All these roles we mentioned should come out into the open during the engagement period. It helps to verbalize your concept of life beforehand, for you will want to mask what is your true self if it doesn't seem to fit into the role you think your fiancé wants. It is in this way that many girls feel frustrated. The demands of modern life are too taxing to add the burden of playing roles. It is impossible to carry it off. Sooner or later your husband will find you out or you will collapse from playing the game and then you will have to start anew in rebuilding your unity. Look at yourself now. If you are not all you would like to be, then try changing yourself. It is easy now that you are young. You are not yet set in your ways nor are you engaged and so hopelessly involved with your love that you can't discuss these concepts.

This is where developing the skills to communicate are vital. Right now is the time to get these skills. How can you get them? We recommend in all seriousness taking a course in discussion and in semantics. If you can't take formal courses then pick up an elementary book in each subject and read it thoroughly. Discussion essentially involves intelligent listening and intelligent responding. For wives this is invaluable. Semantics can save a husband from disaster. It's not what your wife says it, it is how she says it. You are going to be talking about everything from the garbage disposal to your intimate moments of love in order to keep the life blood flowing into your marriage. It seems only logical, then, to learn how to talk and how to listen. Companies today are spending millions of dollars just to give these skills to their employees so business will run smoothly. Shouldn't you give your marriage the same high rating? Good communication frees you from nagging guilt about anything, brings stupid trivia out into the open, clears the air and helps you know each other better. These skills, with tact and a sense of humor, go hand in hand. If you can't laugh, even your wedding night can be a disaster.

In-laws, money and politics can break your back if you don't know how to laugh. It's taken us three and one-half years and a barrel of quarrels and tears to learn this fact. After all, you are leaving your families. Their ways are not the only ways of doing things. You especially have to remember this when the children come. Money is another troublemaker. A wife should always have a little money of her own to squander. We've gotten it up to $2.00 a week already. It helps the wife make the transition from having her own salary, or substantial allowance, to the dependence she will experience upon her husband's salary. If you girls work after marriage you should try to work out a good policy about your salary as soon as you can. We don't believe a wife's salary should be used for everyday luxuries e.g. extensive nightclubbing, steak three times a week, expensive wines and so on. It is much more fun to work up to these luxuries on your husband's salary alone. Let your salary start a home fund or a trip fund or an education fund. A wife's salary can be a very touchy subject.

A husband, on the other hand, shouldn't make a wife feel guilty if she doesn't really want to work. A young woman needs the luxurious days before children come to devote herself entirely to her husband and homemaking. Regarding money, we think you may be tempted to over-romanticize the struggling marriage where the husband is working for a degree while the wife works to put him through. It is a rough road and demands real maturity because you will not be leading the same existence. After the goal of education has been achieved, some couples have found that without the struggle binding them together their marriage hasn't much depth at all.

We've been talking pretty much about the mundane things which can crack a marriage. But what of the essentials? For us, the most important thing is to discuss and formulate a mutual understanding about the sacrament of marriage and your future common spiritual life. On your wedding day you will be communicating to one another your vows of love and fidelity. So many times today we hear from every age group "What's the difference. You buy a marriage license, go to the priest or the J.P., and boom, everything becomes legal. One day it's a sin, the next day a virtue." Right?? Why get married before a priest, why in fact legalize marriage at all? Isn't it all rather hypocritical? Can a $3.00 piece of paper make a difference?

TURN ON—TUNE IN—DROP OUT

Turning on: One of the cries of the psychedelic movement is that we should return to the mystical, to our tribal instincts. There is no better mystical concept than the joining of two people, body and soul, into one. The wedding ceremony itself, in one form or another, for all peoples has been a tribal ritual full of the symbols of life and death. Hence we hear the admonitions about "for richer or for poorer, etc." These have linked the ancient to the present. Over the years the symbols such as the rings, the dress, the formality, have acquired meanings in themselves, as well as the meanings they originally had: purity, fidelity, seriousness. Now these symbols are part of our Judeo-Christian ritual of marriage which will continue to evolve and be passed on to our children and their children. To take part in these rituals is not hypocritical. It is human to want to link yourself with past generations, whether or not this desire is fully recognized. These are but brief looks at the historical whys of the need for a marriage ceremony. More important, the sacrament of marriage is a spiritual act, and unless you can deny the existence of the spiritual altogether, you will visualize in your mind's eye what this sacrament is and its effect. When you marry you give the ultimate love-gift, yourself, totally, forever. A portion of this gift, the sexual act, which everyone seems to worry about being illegal one day and legal the next, is the final completion of the marriage ritual. Any ritual of importance is performed publicly with the approval of the tribe and witnesses and with a solemnity and reverence for the consequences. We are not advocating large, expensive weddings when we say this, but this act of marrying is a fulfillment of your humanness. What else have we left in this computerized age?

This may strike you as rather wild, but we think that until you can truly see together the symbol-laden ritual of marrying, you won't see the real why's of marrying in church before a priest at a nuptial Mass. Nor will you realize what Christ did to this ritual when he made it a sacrament. You must turn on with the sacrament of marriage; in it contemplate the vows of love and fidelity and realize the direct line you have to graces from God and the mutual assistance, sexually and mentally, you will get from each other which will nurture this truly mystical union. On a more romantic note, you should think, and rightly so, that with the proper individual preparation you are star-crossed lovers like those in the movie "Black Orpheus," destined and loved by God.

Now if you are turned on you must tune in. The individual you must tune in to is the new you of marriage. You have to continue to tune in to the wavelength you and your mate established during your engagement and above all you must tune in to God. It is very hard to be married without some sort of prayer-life. You won't believe it, but things really do look better and become better with prayer, because essentially our prayer is that we will change, that we will give, that we will create calm and security and understanding. Before marriage we sort of pray that our loved one will change, that we will be happy, that we will be loved—essentially selfish prayers. You tune in also to the giving of your love-gifts in this love-in. These are honest gifts. The sexual act becomes a true communication in itself—one means of binding wounds and grievances. When you tune in to your state of life as it is, you bind yourself to your beloved fully in your vows of love and fidelity.

What about dropping out? This can be the hardest act of all. It requires constant vigilance and it can become quite a game. First you must drop out of your respective families as daughter and son and return as the married couple (a united front against the world in more romantic terms). It is easy to want to cling to the dependence and security you are fighting against now after you marry and find that another person is now solely dependent on you. It is much easier at the very beginning of marriage, we have found, kindly but fiercely, to guard your privacy and seclusion. You can always let up gradually, but it is hard to start once patterns of interference have been set. Wives especially have to remember they are no longer "Daddy's little girl." For example, we didn't have a telephone for the first three months of our marriage. We lived near our parents and wanted to be alone; not having to explain our every move, or be available constantly to the family. Now we have a happy balance of shared friendship. Second, you have to drop from real social competition, indeed from strict social groups if they devour you. It is easy to envy. You know that as teenagers. It eats at you and you are miserable. Acquire things, whether new or old, slowly. We still hunt out good-looking used furniture to go with our few new pieces. It's fun and draws us closer together by making everything we own have a story for us to remember together. Wanting something is almost more fun than having it. When you get something you want, something precious goes out of your life and you must fill the void with appreciation of it and with another desire. We say this because we could have afforded a phone, TV, much furniture from the start of our marriage but we didn't want to deny ourselves the joy of building a home together. In a sense even our old refinished furniture represents love gifts. It isn't easy to get this detachment, especially if you really can't afford anything but second-hand furniture. It doesn't sound like fun. It sounds like being poor and shabby and dull. But the riches this type of building can bring to your marriage you cannot buy. You have only one beginning to your marriage and you will want to look back in five, twenty, and thirty years on this beginning and love it. Whether you are wealthy or not you will be glad that those years set the tone of "dropping out" for the rest.

This doesn't mean you have to drop out of working toward your potential, financial and otherwise. We think it is important to drop out of the rat-race mentality. It means dropping out of the "beautiful people" syndrome with all its ramifications of the "right" things to do, to see, to go to, etc. These things aren't wrong in themselves of course, but watch your motivations. Wanting to be "in" in whatever milieu you find yourself can be devastating. It can encourage you to give up little pin-size bits of your integrity and begin to eat at the core of honesty between you. Learn now to develop this drop-out attitude by assessing the whys of what you are doing. With this ability you can really be honest with your husband and your children. In today's cliché, you at least won't suffer from a credibility gap.

We've talked about communication, the love-in, the turn-on, tune-in, drop-out idea. Shall we get practical and give a few ideas on how to prepare for all of this. Naturally for a life as great as married life there should be some professionalism in preparation. Marriage is not an escape. Thoes who marry young, or who are immature, or who marry to escape will find a life at best tolerable, and very probably stifling. There are always exceptions to which you may point, but we have found that though we were well prepared, had had freedom, had travelled, had an education, there are still times when we want to escape this life, even though these times are few and far between. They constitute no real threat to the fabric of our marriage for they are normal. However, for the ill-prepared young couple entering marriage these feelings may be the rule. The "I could have beens" come more and more often to mind.

In today's competitive world the man must have a means of support and a potential. This means an education. Think for a minute if you had to support a wife on a summer salary—if you were lucky enough to get a job last summer. Also, staying in school may help you stay single longer. Remember you will not be the same person at 28 that you are, or think you are now. Along with having a job and potential goes being happy with your work; this puts the potential aspect into focus. It is important to you, as well as your wife, that you are satisfied with your work, whatever it is. It is much harder to drop out of the system if the old $$$'s keep dogging you into things you don't want to do. You don't want to be a man who feels trapped by his job, by the paycheck it brings in for his family. Who would you blame for this situation? Give yourself some time to be single, to switch around, to develop a true desire for a home of your own, a wife and a concept of yourself as a husband.

For some of you young ladies the responsibilities of wife have been somewhat ground into you; for some of you we suggest you run the house for your mother for a week. We're not joking; it will be a lively experience and you'll discover being a housewife is a profession because it involves people and home-building. This entails cooking, cleaning and serving ad infinitum but it doesn't mean slavery. If you have had experience in homemaking, it won't take you all day to clean a dirty stove and you won't have a nervous breakdown when your in-laws come for dinner. Knowing how to care for an apartment or a house leaves you free to assume the more important work of creating a home. Creating a home your husband is eager to return to is the most continually rewarding experience you have as a homemaker. For you are the center of that home and it is thrilling when your husband comes home day after day wanting to share his day with you. It's up to you to create the intelligent ear and quiet in his life. We can't understand wives who don't want to know what is going on in their husband's world during the day, or for that matter, husbands who refuse to tell their wives about their work. If you establish this openness and sharing of experiences early in marriage you will find genuine friendship and love growing. You will be truly the best of friends.

We have left until last your practical spiritual preparation which is the same for every state in life. A meaningful relationship with God, as well as the pursuit of the aims of Vatican II, will deepen your engagement period and the ultimate love-in. All of us are working toward that ultimate love-in—union with God. If this is your perspective you will have no trouble with the complexities and frustrations of life which you are bound to encounter. You won't sell yourself out and you won't sell out your beloved.

We do want to add another item—your children. They are truly gifts of love from both of you to each other and to God. Personally we have found in our marriage that the concept of responsible parenthood is not a panacea but brings with it the burden of squaring parenthood with unselfishness. If you are living with the drop-out attitude we seem to be hammering at you, your unselfishness will be more clearly able to function honestly in your own particular situation.

Finally, we two struggling, happy people can say to you, "Take a look at your parents as husband and wife. What kind of marriage is it (be charitable but honest)? What would you change and how? What can you learn and what will you take with you and why? What attitudes? What ideals? We challenge you. Plan and work to make your marriage a beautiful LOVE-IN.

A DISSERTATION ON HOMECOMING

It's all big time you see,
(for we are striving to be big time
   aren't we?)
A whole week of waiting, and pressing
excitement

UP 67 — OSU 61

That was the game
They are good
Are we better
Naturalism
does not allow for
good or better

I am a yell leader
2,000 people yelled
and screamed.
People who reside in
Portland cheered with
us. we were not alone
(for once)

I am in love with a
basketball team that
has defeated the #8
team in the nation
and won homecoming

They have lost all the rest
They are real
They only do the bare necessities

Maybe the cheerleaders
were instrumental in
that victory

                                    Chris Lucey

6

TALK TO ME, DAD

Pat and Patty Crowley

When our son, Patrick, was about 17, he and a friend cajoled Pat into accompanying them to the local dragstrip one Sunday. A fair enough project, Pat thought. But the ultimate test came when it was decided Dad should make a run in the dragster. A quick observation convinced Pat it was mainly necessary to race the motor incessantly and loudly. As he did this at the starting line, he killed the engine, wasn't able to restart it, and had to be towed away—humiliation. Perhaps the afternoon did little to bridge the generation gap, perhaps it did much.

The incident reminds us that our son frequently sees the world, regardless of the layers of cynicism he sometimes puts on as part of his pose, as essentially a green and good place. Father very often, despite the optimistic terminology he may sometimes adopt as part of *his* pose, must mingle his optimism with a sense of death, sin and corruption that the youngster cannot possibly understand until he has lived a few more years. Any appreciation of communication between parents and children, it seems to us, must begin with this essentially realistic way of looking at the fact; i.e., that we are different generations and that very fact will make communication—the kind of open-hearted, completely understanding, unhesitating communication that we all seek—difficult, but happily, not impossible.

It has become fashionable to bemoan the inability of the members of different generations to communicate with each other. The "misunderstood teen-ager" syndrome is an example of this fact. We forget that the very term "teen-ager" is hardly a generation old. In the day of our parents the concept of a teen-ager would not have been grasped. He would have been looked upon as an adolescent, a person who is going through the awkward age, as a person somewhere between childhood and maturity. But the possibility that he is a special kind of human being with a special set of problems that enabled him, as a teen-ager, to communicate with his kind better than with his parents is a concept that would have mystified our mothers and fathers. Yet in our culture, today, the teen-ager does have this coherent, homogeneous mass self-identity by which each individual within his group measures himself. He sees himself as a unique person. The phrase "my generation" or "my music" is said with the clear-cut meaning that "mine" is substantially in its essences different from "yours." The teen who prefers "my" kind of music and sees it as an identifying mark of a generation in itself, creates problems of communication that did not exist 25 years ago.

We are also becoming a nation of young people. This fact is convulsing our economy. It is affecting our advertising. It is studied in our TV studios. Indeed, today's mercantile world rests upon the concept that the buyer is a young person and it is his needs which must be satisfied. It is the very young person, especially the girl, who is setting style fashions. A few years ago daughter imitated mother as soon as she was old enough in style and fashion. Now daughter sets the styles and mother follows suit, provided she can afford it.

Through mass media, there are many outsiders who now speak directly to the child in a way not possible 20 years ago. The child who today goes to sleep with a transistor radio under his pillow is being inculcated with a set of values and a way of looking at the world that may be contrary to the way mother and father see it. We do not suggest parents cannot affect the child's values—in fact, they can and must, but we want to guard against the easy simplification that somehow love and understanding on the part of parents will automatically bring about communication. Love and understanding alone may not; there are too many voices, too many intervening influences that makes the parent's job more difficult than ever before.

The vast network of radio and TV helps persuade the adolescent that he is a fundamentally different kind of person. They flatter and they sympathize. As one headline put it recently, speaking directly to youngsters, "Misunderstood Teen-Agers: A Column for You." The writer did not reflect that perhaps all teenagers are not misunderstood or that there may be some who do not feel they are misunderstood. He merely participated in the stereotypical view; if you are a teenager, you are misunderstood.

An essential fact we cannot overlook is that the responsibility of opening channels of communication rests with the parents. Although they have obstacles to overcome, they cannot shirk the fact that what happens in their families depends largely on who they are, how they see their children, the world, and how they see God.

It is an important part of a parent's job to listen intently; doing so, he will communicate in a way that may transcend any words he may possibly use. What was it Emerson said? "I cannot hear what you are saying, because what you are speaks so loudly." It is commonplace to say that the parents' words mean little if they are not essentially what reinforces what the parent is and is becoming. If the parent is unable to back up his words, unable to be the kind of person his noble words suggest he wants his child to become, his actions will smother any effect his words might have.

The home is the central force in shaping a youngster's way of looking at the world; a fact that has always been at the center of the Christian Family Movement and that in recent years has been abundantly confirmed. For example, Father Andrew Greeley and his associates at the National Opinion Research Center concluded, after a massive study of Catholic schools, that the school is able to have maximum impact upon the students only when the school work is an extension of what takes place in the home. We do not suggest that is the only conclusion emerging from this report, but it was one that impressed us particularly. Similarly, we see in the Office of Economic Opportunity, the War on Poverty, that increasing attention must be paid to the kind of family life taking place in a poverty-stricken home. Virtually the whole thrust of the War on Poverty is an effort to establish conditions to make a human home life possible. In the Head Start program, the good work of a few hours every day is not able to overcome and counteract a home environment that may be poverty-ridden, fatherless and chaotic.

Styles of life and communication will be different from one home to the next. We doubt if anyone can set down "rules" by which every family will advance communication by using words alone. We know some families are happiest in an environment that might best be described as "pandemonium." We have seen other families can best communicate when they get things off their chest; even when they shout and argue, they know they love each other and that their words of intensity will not be mistaken. Other families will be shattered by a word louder than the speech patterns ordinarily used.

Recreations of families also differ. Financial condition will play a part in its recreation activities, as does its size. A father of 12, whom we know, strives to spend an occasional half-hour alone with each child, because he understands that at a fundamental level of the child's life, he finds comfort and happiness in being alone with his parent. It is dangerous to praise one style over another. Our own style of life has not been such that many would think it conducive to communication. Our many visitors, frequent travels, preoccupation with the Christian Family Movement and its activities, as well as business and family routines that engage us would ordinarily be thought to impede communication. But, we have found that this is often the way we come to good terms with each other and with our children.

In the life of the Church many theologians, teachers and priests who work with young people are agreed that communicating with them must be based on treating them as "whole" persons. We must speak to their intellects as well as their emotions. We must persuade and talk with and guide rather than issue decrees. We can no longer simply tell a youngster he should be pure because it is a sin to be otherwise. We must put this moral precept into a context that will make sense to him as a human being. We must talk with him about the meaning of being a whole person, a person of integrity who understands and possesses himself so he, in turn, may some day be able to give himself to another.

The best communication will take place when the family works together in a common cause. It does little good, for example, to lecture a youngster about the evils of racial hatred if one does little to overcome the prejudice that exists in the world. Many people would never dream of saying an impolite word to a black man but would also never dream of permitting him to live in their neighborhood. Young people are able to see the actions of parents with a blinding clarity. They know a phoney when they see one. This kind of relationship in a family, no matter what the other happy circumstances, inevitably leads to breakdown of communication.

We recall an essay in *Time* that described a family that worked together in a center for drug addicts. Other families bring their older children to help tutor the disadvantaged. The youngster who works with his parents distributing political literature or helping migrant laborers is part of a network of loving communication that can't be surpassed. It depends on action and words.

7

REACH OUT MY PEOPLE

Dr. Willis and Genevieve McNelly

Television, transistor radios, hi-fi, walkie talkies and Strobe lights—we've been subjected, cajoled, nauseated and thrilled by these electronic gadgets at one time or another. We live in the era of the communication media.

These things are gifts from man to man and the electronic revolution is here to stay. It belongs to the new generation and their children; it is for all of us to enjoy. Such a vast world of communications must lead us to come close together, to converse with one another, to understand and enjoy our fellowman.

We also live in a frenzied, fast-paced age. Concentration is all but impossible; noise pollution may eventually keep us from hearing "conventional" sounds. Learning how to dialogue, how to listen, has already been sacrificed far too often. In spite of our vast resources of communication skills, we probably have more loneliness, misunderstanding, alienation, isolation, than ever before in history. For example, we have the breakdown of family life, the growing lack of understanding between generations, distorted attitudes toward minority rights and resistance to political and religious change.

The fear of being "separate" or "alone" haunts us all. Every man needs to be cared about, loved, wanted, appreciated. Man is, after all, a social animal. A personal union with another lights up the world inside us; man remains alone, alienated, unwanted without this love. Separateness can be overcome *only* by love. When God created us in His image, He meant us to become involved with others, as he had with us.

Father Philip Berrigan says well: "The opposite of love is not hatred; it is indifference. When we have learned indifference, when we are really skilled and determined at the business of ignoring others, of putting our own well-being, our own options first—of thrusting our own ego into life, as the ideal form of life itself—we may be quite certain that at that point, life has become hell. We need be no more thoroughly damned."

The great need people have is not satisfied by "things." Life becomes meaningful when we share with others their joys, interests, sorrow, anxiety, humor and fears. It is obvious that, surrounded as we are by electronic information, the desire to communicate is more of a reality to man today than it has ever been, and yet we may well remain only on the superficial level of knowledge. We may never penetrate the exciting, stimulating interior life of ourselves or others; never achieve a vital relationship with other human beings. Concentration—whether it be listening to music, reading, talking to a person, seeing the living world around us—is often sacrificed for superficialities.

If one is "concentrated" it really matters very little what the object of concentration is, as long as it's outside of self. Giving one's whole attention is giving one's heart. This kind of attention is what Christ meant when he spoke of having "ears that hear and eyes that see." To concentrate means to live fully in the present, to tune in, to turn on. It is an art to be cultivated.

Search for truth about another person occurs when being and truth in one individual confronts being and truth in another. This interchange is called DIA-LOGUE. It is not always easy or comfortable to achieve but when successful, an encounter with another human being is experienced. We see the other, hear the other, so that the reality outside of ourselves has been felt as though it were ours.

God created man to desire union, to be known, to be loved, and to love. These desires are common to all, but many of us would rather suffer separateness and loneliness than risk the attempt to reach out to another person, to hear what he has to say. Because of our absorption in ourselves, we may fear rejection. On the other hand, some people are so egocentric, so rigid, that they keep the timid from ever revealing their inward selves to anyone. To know a person is to know God as well, for He said He would not be found if He was not first seen in our neighbor. Much of the current dissatisfaction with theology and the idea that God is "dead" comes from the lack of evidence that man has any love for man. Surely, they say, if man is dead to love, there is no God. And, where else is man to find witness for the love God has for man unless men permit love to radiate from the love they have for each other.

Love comes through dialogue. Love is not something that "comes" before talking, nor as a sensation or novelty—love emerges in the mutual awareness and delight in the wonder and beauty of the other person's mind and heart. In dialogue, the one who loves yearns to love, to understand, to exchange with the other his thoughts, needs, joys. This sharing is indispensable to our mental health, our spiritual development, our own reality. People need people. "We must love one another, or die!" says poet W. H. Auden.

Everywhere in this 20th century, men are coming together to talk to one another. The United Nations is an example where men convene to engage in dialogue, to listen. Pope Paul, himself, came to the UN to plead, "No more war! No more war!" In business and industry, management and labor, in ecumenical and interfaith exchanges the persons involved in dialogue are the better for it. These dialogues engender openness, concentration, a willingness to suspend judgment, to *listen*.

From your own experience you know a good teacher not only imparts knowledge, he grows in teaching ability to the degree he listens to the students as they share their insights from the world in which they live. Such a teacher relates to the students and they to him. The Church has learned she must dialogue and redialogue with each decade of young adults, with each generation and the various peoples of the world. She must speak, not only with her own people, but with all men. The people of God, the Church, meets the needs of people by listening to people. In this dialogue the Church stays abreast, is renewed, refreshed.

Without dialogue, community in the Church is only an abstraction. The people of God cannot grow in love for one another with listening.

Communication, though, is not easy. Reality has difficulty keeping up with the ideal. Differences occur among neighbors, between husband and wife, brothers and sisters, parents and child. If we hope to get out of our personal ghettos we must acquire some knowledge of the dynamics of personal relationships.

It is naive to believe that because one can talk, he

can communicate. Many people who think dialogue and communication is easy can end up in a desperate argument when confronted with frustrating or conflicting points of view. They raise their voices, avoid the subject, sulk or even come to blows. The root of all these poor responses to dialogue is ignorance.

Of all the barriers to dialogue the misuse of language is probably the greatest. Its use or abuse can be a soothing experience or an emotionally charged one. Our words are neither exact nor precise; many of our meanings, for example, are badly outdated. Students who have struggled with Shakespeare's prose know how almost meaningless some words are today. Also, the same word can mean different things to different people. A "pad" is one thing to a hippie, another to a foot specialist, and something totally different to a rocket expert.

We can acquire preconceived images or distortions about many people. Expecting people to act in stereotyped ways prevents them from being themselves with us and keeps us from knowing them as they really are. Bias and prejudice are attitudes born from conditioning and ignorance, not reality.

Psychological difficulties also prevent understanding. Some people don't listen because truth is tough. Some have such an exalted notion of their superiority they block off communication, some fear attack. Some persons are compulsive talkers; they may be afraid to listen. Teachers, parents and ministers may be so preoccupied with what they have to say they rarely recognize that their listeners need to converse and share their world.

Most difficulties in dialogue, we believe, are due to emotional psychological reactions and the abuse of words. Tone of voice, facial and bodily gestures and personal idiosyncrasies also communicate, but it is not "how" a person is speaking but "what" he is trying to say that is important. Behind the words used the conceptual life of man exists. "My God, it was all my life, and it was the only material I had," said F. Scott Fitzgerald about his writing.

When communication happens one "sees" with the eyes of another, "hears" with the ears of another, "wears the shoes" of another. Only as we come to know another and are also known by him can we understand what it means to have full Christian maturity.

We need great teachers of dialogue to teach others. Life is exciting because people are exciting. This is the final miracle of which Reuel Howe writes: "Miracles of dialogue are needed in all relationships, individual, social, educational, religious, economic, political, national and international. By dialogue we can let God into our world because in dialogue we open ourselves to God. When man is open to man and God, miracles have to happen. But they are forged out of everyday events, the happenings between persons; the conflicts, failures, misunderstands and tragedies of living together, as well as out of the love and acceptance that are both the source and the environment for the working of the miracles of dialogue." [1]

[1] Reuel L. Howe, *The Miracle of Dialogue* (New York: Seabury Press 1963).